This book b

If found, please contact me at:

mithmoth

Made in the USA
Middletown, DE
11 May 2022

65623413R00073